The Issues of Life

A 30-Day Devotional for Women
Offering Faith-Based Help for
Common Struggles

Trina Carson

Copyright © 2022 All rights reserved.

No part of this book may be used or reproduced by any means, graphic, electronic, or mechanical, including photocopying, recording, taping, or by any information storage retrieval system, without the written permission of the publisher except in the case of brief quotations embodied in critical articles and reviews.

ISBN: 979-8-8390-2476-2

Independently Published
First Edition

Cover Art by Keira Burton

All Scripture quotations are taken from the Authorized King James Version of the Bible.

Contents

Lesson 1: You've Hit the Bottom; Now Look Up 6
Lesson 2: Shock/Unbelief 9
Lesson 3: Disappointment 11
Lesson 4: Anger and Bitterness 14
Lesson 5: Loneliness 17
Lesson 6: Discouragement 20
Lesson 7: Dealing with Hopelessness and Suicidal Thoughts 23
Lesson 8: Fear 26
Lesson 9: Regret 30
Lesson 10: How to Get and Stay on Top Side 33
Lesson 11: Maximizing Your Time
    (Making Your Days Count) 37
Lesson 12: Overcoming Shame and Guilt 41
Lesson 13: Dealing With Pride 44
Lesson 14: Helplessness 47
Lesson 15: Dealing with Being Judged 50
Lesson 16: Are You Overwhelmed? 53
Lesson 17: Getting the Load Off Your Back 57
Lesson 18: Attacking Panic Before It Attacks You 60
Lesson 19: The God of Hope 63
Lesson 20: Emotional Roller Coasters 66
Lesson 21: Gossip 70
Lesson 22: When Life Isn't Fair (Dealing with Injustices) 74
Lesson 23: Dealing with Grief 78

Lesson 24: What to Do When Your Life Has No Purpose 81
Lesson 25: Resisting Temptation 85
Lesson 26: Dealing with Mental Trauma from
   Past Experiences 89
Lesson 27: The Blame Game 93
Lesson 28: Don't Come Whining to Me! 97
Lesson 29: How to Handle Rejection 100
Lesson 30: Overcoming Issues with Self-Esteem 103
Bonus Lesson: Keeping Your Relationship with God Strong .. 107
Suggested Bible Reading 111
About the Author 112

This 30-day devotional addresses many issues that women face each day. There are 30 different topics that are given. Each topic then gives biblical helps that can give lasting victory.

Many of the ideas presented here have been areas of struggle for me personally. Since the Bible is our guidebook, we can look to it for sure answers.

All references in this book are from the King James Version of the Bible (KJV). You will greatly benefit by using this version, as there are many exercises you will need to write out based on the KJV. If you are unsure of where to find a passage, look in the front of the Bible for the listing of all the books and this will help you find the verses.

Each lesson is based on different topics that will be helpful to you. The layout presents many of the struggles you have faced or will face. Each lesson concludes with daily reading as well as a brief exercise to reinforce the subject matter. Feel free to do the lessons in order or if you are struggling in a certain area, do that lesson on that topic for that given day.

It is my prayer that this book will offer you hope, something you may be lacking at this point. If you follow the truths given from the Bible, you will find an abundance of help and encouragement from the God who loves you unconditionally.

Today you get to decide: am I a victim or a victor? A victim can't do anything about their situation. A victor can totally control the situation and come out better on the other side. This book is designed to help you become a victor. Allow God to take what you've experienced and use it to better yourself and to enable you to help others. God can use what you are currently going through to work for good in your life.

My pastor uses an illustration that I'd like to share with you. What would it taste like to eat a spoonful of flour? How about a spoonful of baking powder, baking soda, or lard? None of these sound like pleasant options individually. They would taste awful. But combine them all together in the correct amounts, shape them, and bake them in the oven. You will soon get to enjoy some yummy biscuits.

The same is true of your life. Many of the things you experience are very distasteful and undesirable, but let God work them all for good, and your life will have a beautiful outcome.

Before you begin, more importantly than reading this book and getting help from it is knowing for sure where you will spend your eternity. If you died today, do you know for sure that you would go to Heaven or would you have a doubt?

What do you think someone would have to do to go to Heaven? It doesn't matter what I think or really what you think. It only matters what God says.

Here is what God says we must know, understand, and accept to be saved.

We Must Realize We Are All Sinners

For all have sinned, and come short of the glory of God (Romans 3:23).

No one is perfect. I have told at least one lie in my life, and because you probably have as well, that means both of us are sinners. The first point is that simple: we are all sinners.

We Must Believe There Is a Price to Be Paid for Our Sins

For the wages of sin is death; but the gift of God is eternal life through Jesus Christ our Lord (Romans 6:23).

And death and hell were cast into the lake of fire. This is the second death (Revelation 20:14).

There is a price we deserve to pay for our sin. If I get caught speeding, then I get a ticket. If I get caught robbing a bank, then I am going to jail. If I get caught killing someone, then I could get the death penalty. The Bible says the price (wage) for sin is death. We deserve to die because of our sin. This is more than just a physical death, but it is a spiritual death in a place called the lake of fire. God says even liars will be there.

But the fearful, and unbelieving, and the abominable, and murderers, and whoremongers, and sorcerers, and idolaters, and all liars, shall have their part in the lake which burneth with fire and brimstone: which is the second death (Revelation 21:8).

We Must Believe Jesus Died, Was Buried, and Arose from the Dead to Pay the Price for Our Sins

But God commendeth His love toward us in that while we were yet sinners, Christ died for us (Romans 5:8).

Jesus showed us how much He loved us by dying on the cross for us. He literally took our place and paid our hell for us.

Imagine if your best friend killed someone and got the death penalty, and you offered to take his place. Your guilty friend would go free, and you would be put to death in his place. That is what Jesus did for us. We are sinners, and He is perfect; yet He died on the cross to pay our hell for us.

We Must Believe Salvation Does Not Come by Our Works, but Only by Putting Our Faith and Trust in Christ and What He Did for Us on the Cross

For by grace are ye saved through faith; and that not of yourselves: it is the gift of God: Not of works, lest any man should boast (Ephesians 2:8-9).

But to him that worketh not, but believeth on him that justifieth the ungodly, his faith is counted for righteousness (Romans 4:5).

Many people are trying to get to Heaven by their good works and good deeds. No matter how good their works are, good works will not get them to Heaven. Only trusting Jesus as their Saviour will save them.

We Must Believe That If We Put Our Trust in Christ Alone, We Can Be Saved

For whosoever shall call upon the name of the Lord shall be saved (Romans 10:13).

If you understand and believe these facts, you can be saved from an eternity in hell. Simply put your faith and trust in Jesus and ask Him to save you. If you would like to be saved, pray this prayer right now, trusting only in Jesus to save you. The prayer itself will not save you, but a prayer is your way of calling on God to save you. You must believe and trust Him in your heart.

Dear Jesus, I know that I am a sinner, and I know that I deserve Hell. Jesus, please save me and take me to Heaven when I die. Jesus, I trust only you as my way to Heaven. Amen.

If by praying that prayer you placed your faith in Christ as your only hope for salvation, then according to the Bible, you are saved. The Spirit of God has entered your heart, and all your sins are forgiven.

LESSON 1

You've Hit the Bottom; Now Look Up

Many times, when a store is preparing to go out of business, they will try to get rid of as much inventory as possible. They will often advertise that their merchandise is at "rock bottom pricing." We all want the prices of things we want to be as low as possible, so seeing an ad like this is very enticing.

But what about when your life hits rock bottom? When things are already bad, but they seem to get worse? When you know for a fact that things couldn't possibly get worse, and then they do.

So here you are. You've hit rock bottom. Where do you go from here? If things in your life have taken a turn for the worse, how do you get things turned around?

God often uses our darkness to bring about good. It is at those moments when everything is going wrong and our lives are falling apart that He finally gets our attention. We may have ignored His pleadings and pushed Him away, but now that we're at the bottom, looking up is our only way out.

Psalm 71:20 says, *Thou, which hast shewed me great and sore troubles, shalt quicken me again, and shalt bring me up again from the depths of the earth.* God can take the trouble that comes in our lives and use it to get us close to Him so He can help us get back up again.

Who do you turn to when you're in trouble? Friends, drugs, alcohol? These are not good sources. You need help from above. 2

Chronicles 15:4 says, *But when they in their trouble did turn unto the LORD God of Israel, and sought him, he was found of them.* If you've ever sought the Lord, you need to seek Him now.

Psalm 72:12 says, *For he shall deliver the needy when he crieth; the poor also, and him that hath no helper.* Are you needy? Cry out to the Lord for His help. God can deliver you. This doesn't mean being delivered from the consequences of your actions. This means He can deliver you from a lifestyle that is causing you to go down the wrong path.

You may have no one to help you right now. Why don't you get close to God and let Him work in your life? He can change the course of your life and guide your life down a path of blessing.

Think of trying to awaken a heavy sleeper. God knows exactly what it takes to wake us up. Some are harder to wake up than others. For some, it may take a firm jolt, where God must rock our world. Others who are sensitive to His call may only require a gentle shake. Be quick to respond to the Lord when He is trying to get your attention.

Since you're at the bottom, look up! Consider this verse in Psalm 121:1: *I will lift up mine eyes unto the hills, from whence cometh my help.* You can get help from the Lord. Though Satan has worked hard to destroy your life, God wants to give you an abundant life. You may be at the bottom now, but if you allow the Lord to help you, you can make it to the top!

Daily Reading

John 10:10; Isaiah 55:6; Psalm 120:1

Psalm 40:2 – *He _____ me up also out of an _____ _____, out of the miry clay, and set my _____ upon a _____, and _____ my _____.*

LESSON 2

Shock/Unbelief

Have you ever had one of those moments when things are so bad that you hoped with all that is you in that this is just a bad dream–perhaps even a nightmare? You may pinch yourself and shake yourself in hopes that you will snap out of it, but the reality of it is, this **is** your reality. No matter how much you try to escape it, there is no denying your current scenario.

Your life may be at its lowest point ever. Your mind can't even begin to process your current situation.

In spite of the mental state you are in, there is hope! All of us face low points in our lives. It is often our lows that lead us to great heights in our lives. You are in a prime position to receive help from the Lord. Consider the verse in the Bible: *The LORD preserveth the simple: I was brought low, and he helped me* (Psalm 116:6).

In this passage, David thought he was going to die. You may think you'd rather die than to be where you are, facing what you are up against. However, hitting bottom puts you in the perfect spot for receiving help from God! Often God uses low times in our lives to give us the help we need. Take the circumstances you are going through and allow God to help you turn your trial into triumph.

Daily Reading

Psalm 116:1-9

Which verse in this passage encourages you most with your situation? Write this verse out and take time to think about it (meditate) and how it can help you.

LESSON 3

Disappointment

Imagine it's the beginning of a new year. The excitement of the holidays is now behind you. You're excited about a fresh new start. Those extra pounds are going out the window. You've resolved and made plans that this is the year for a new you!

The alarm goes off! You can't believe it's morning already. Where did the time go? Your resolve seems to have died during the night. You hit the snooze—just a few more minutes. Thirty minutes later, you finally roll out of bed and realize you no longer have time for that 30-minute workout. Oh, well . . . maybe tomorrow.

The days slip by and so do your plans and goals for a healthier you. Forget it! *I should have known better than to think I could do this*, you think. *What's the use?* You're deeply disappointed with yourself. You begin thinking back through the dozens of times you've gotten your hopes up only to realize you failed yet again.

Maybe you're in this same state of mind today. You promised your family you were different. You'd hung around that bad crowd for the last time, taken your last hit of drugs and alcohol. Temptation came, and all your hope was stolen. You've disappointed yourself and most definitely your family. You had such good intentions.

How do you survive the shame of the disappointment? The Bible as well as the world around us is filled with people just like

The Issues of Life

you, disappointed in themselves, yet God says there is hope and help for all.

Do you know that God is aware of your weaknesses? He knows everything about you, even your disappointments in yourself. Psalm 103:14 tells us, *For he knoweth our frame; he remembereth that we are dust.* God knows what you are made of. He considers that you are dust and that you are prone to come short of pleasing Him.

Romans 3:23 says, *For all have sinned, and come short of the glory of God.*

No matter how hard you try to do right, you will come short. That doesn't mean you shouldn't try, but rather when you try and fail, you need to be reminded and encouraged to get back up and keep trying.

Proverbs 24:16 reminds us, *For a just man falleth seven times, and riseth up again: but the wicked shall fall into mischief.* Even when you are trying your hardest and you fail, get back up and determine to do right. God will help you get the victory you are seeking.

Daily Reading

Romans 7:15-25

Consider verse 15: *For that which I do I _____ not: for what I would, that do I not; but what I _____, that do I.*

Paul is telling about his own struggles with sin. This is the common struggle of easily doing the things we don't need to do while doing the things we should avoid.

Verse 18 says, *For I know that in me (that is, in my _____,) dwelleth ____ _____ _____: for to will is present with me; but _____ to _____ that which is _____ I find not.*

Verse 24 asks the question, *_____ shall _____ me?*

The hope is found in verse 25, which says, *I thank God through Jesus Christ our Lord.* This is the believer's hope for the disappointments we bring upon ourselves. It is only through Christ that we can experience victory in this life.

LESSON 4

Anger and Bitterness

What if you found out today that there was a parasite living in your body that was eating your vital organs away at a very rapid pace? I think each of us would get expert medical help and do everything we could to strictly adhere to the advice that could resolve this situation.

Yet secretly living inside so many is a silent killer. This hidden destroyer is anger and bitterness. These have the capacity to kill without you ever even being aware of the danger of its existence inside you.

Perhaps you've been hurt by someone and that has contributed to your current circumstances. You may have just been in the wrong place at the wrong time, and now you are faced with hardship. You couldn't even dream of forgiving the person who has wronged you. You'd rather take that wrong to the grave with you.

Unresolved anger and unforgiveness about wrongs you have experienced will only serve to hurt you while the other person goes merrily on their way. Choosing not to biblically deal with these issues will lead to bitterness, which can be extremely troubling for you.

Let's see how the Bible tells us to deal with these hardships. Ephesians 4:31-32 tells us: *Let all bitterness, and wrath, and anger, and clamour, and evil speaking, be put away from you, with all malice: And be ye kind one to another, tenderhearted, forgiving one another, even as God for Christ's sake hath forgiven you.*

God commands us to put away bitterness and anger. He also instructs us to forgive one another. When we obey the Lord and forgive those who have wronged us, even if they don't ask us to, we will be amazed at the freedom it will bring.

You will either hang on to things from the past that have hurt you, or you can choose to give these issues to the Lord, allowing Him to help you forgive those who have wronged you.

Don't let the anger and bitterness control you and win in your life. When you choose the path of forgiveness, your spirit will be freer than it has ever been!

Daily Reading

Luke 23:34; Matthew 6:14-15; Genesis 50:15-21

Write out one of these verses that helps you with forgiveness.

LESSON 5

Loneliness

Isn't it interesting how you can be surrounded by people and at the same time be lonely? You can even be in very close quarters with people sitting within arm's reach and still feel all alone. Many people put on a front day after day, pretending to be something they are not in an effort to not be alone. They would rather live a lie than be alone.

At this moment, you may be experiencing loneliness. You may be surrounded by people on a daily basis, whether through work or other social interactions, and yet you still feel all alone.

Sometimes we won't allow people to help us because we think they don't understand what we are going through. Do you know Jesus understands loneliness? At one point, every one of Jesus's disciples left him. Jesus knows exactly what it's like to be lonely. Though the whole world may seem to be against us, for those who have received Him in their hearts, He promises never to leave us. He can give us help through our lonely hours.

Jesus experienced a time when many of His disciples chose to leave Him and not follow Him anymore. John 6:66 says, *From that time many of his disciples went back, and walked no more with him.* This lets us know that Jesus was familiar with loneliness. He knew what it was like to have people turn against Him.

The Issues of Life

Remember that whatever you go through in life, Jesus understands and is able to help you through whatever hardships you face.

Daily Reading:

Isaiah 41:10 – *Fear thou not; for I am with thee: be not dismayed; for I am thy God: I will strengthen thee; yea, I will help thee; yea, I will uphold thee with the right hand of my righteousness.*

Joshua 1:9 – *Have not I commanded thee? Be strong and of a good courage; be not afraid, neither be thou dismayed: for the LORD thy God is with thee whithersoever thou goest.*

Psalm 27:10 – *When my father and my mother forsake me, then the LORD will take me up.*

Write out the following verse that describes how Jesus experienced loneliness.

Matthew 26:5

Take time to pray and tell Jesus all about the emotions of your heart. He cares and can help lift you out of your loneliness.

LESSON 6

Discouragement

Each of us faces times of discouragement in our lives. We anticipate a matter turning out one way and it ends up completely different than what we expected. This can lead us to be discouraged.

Failures can bring on feelings of discouragement. Have you ever taken a test you felt well prepared for, only to find that when you got your grade, you didn't do as well as you thought? You may have even sensed that things were going well even as you were answering the questions on the test. How discouraging it is when the outcome doesn't end like you hoped.

A perfect example of discouragement in the Bible was with the children of Israel. They were in bondage to Pharaoh, king of Egypt. When the Israelites were first told by Moses the Lord's promise to deliver them from their bondage, they bowed their heads and worshipped the Lord. Finally, hope was in sight! Little did they know all that was to come.

When Moses and Aaron went to tell Pharaoh about God's plan to deliver the children of Israel from beneath his bondage, he did not like what they had to say. He made the workload of the Israelites even tougher. The Israelites were not too happy with Moses and Aaron. They were discouraged, and they would face many other forms of discouragement in the years to come.

Being discouraged can cause us to want to withdraw and be in isolation. Is this the biblical way to deal with discouragement? What is the Bible answer for this common problem?

One of the most important things to remember when you're facing discouragement is that the Lord is with you wherever you go. Your family can't always be with you, and those you consider to be friends will disappoint you. Yet if you've accepted Christ as your Savior, He has promised that He is with you.

In the Bible, Joshua 1:9 says, *Have not I commanded thee? Be strong and of a good courage; be not afraid, neither be thou dismayed: for the Lord thy God is with thee whithersoever thou goest.*

This promise offers encouragement and reminds you of the hope that is in Christ. Cling to this promise!

Daily Reading

Psalm 42; 43:5

In three verses from the above passages, the Bible tells us what to do when we are cast down or discouraged. The answer is to _____ in God.

LESSON 7

Dealing with Hopelessness and Suicidal Thoughts

You may be familiar with some of statements listed below. You may have had all of them directed at you personally. They all indicate that you let someone down and they have lost hope in you. You can even mess things up so badly that people tell you that you are a hopeless case.

- "You never do anything right."
- "You're such a loser."
- "Why do you keep doing the same stupid things over and over again?"
- "I should have known. You messed up again."
- "Just get out of my life and don't ever come back again!"

Words like these are extremely painful. They can push you to the point where life becomes hopeless for you. You may have even given it your best shot with trying to do the right thing. Someone may have given you just one more chance and you blew it.

You must recognize that there is an enemy who is after your life. The devil wants to take every one of our lives, and wreck and ruin them. God has given each of us incredible potential, but when the devil messes us up, we are often led to a place of hopelessness.

The Issues of Life

Let's look in God's Word and see what Satan's agenda is for us and find out how we can overcome these feelings of hopelessness that can ultimately steal our desire to live.

John 10:10 says, *The thief cometh not, but for to steal, and to kill, and to destroy: I am come that they might have life, and that they might have it more abundantly.*

Jesus is speaking in this verse. He is talking about the devil's game plan. The devil is a thief. He wants to steal the purpose God has for your life. He's out to steal your family, your future, and anything he can take from you. His goal is to kill and destroy you. Any time you begin to feel hopeless, remember who is behind the hopelessness you feel.

Jesus says His reason for coming was that we might have life. He is never in favor of anyone taking their own life. He is the author and giver of life. He wants us to have an abundant life.

A life lived for Christ is a life with a purpose. It is a blessed and happy life that is lived for God and others. There is **always** hope found in Christ. Romans 15:13 says, *Now the God of hope fill you with all joy and peace in believing, that ye may abound in hope, through the power of the Holy Ghost.*

Daily Reading
Mark 5:25-34

This is the story of a woman who had a health problem for twelve years, who had spent all her money seeking help but only got worse. Read the story to find out the hope she found in Christ.

What did this lady do to find healing for her hopeless situation?

God cares about you in the same way he cared about this woman. After dealing with her situation for twelve years, she probably felt there was no hope for her life. In verse 34 of this passage, Jesus tells the woman *to go in* _____, *and be* _____ *of thy plague.*

It's amazing what can happen when we allow our lives to be touched by the Lord. He is willing and able to give us help when all hope seems gone. Stop now and pray and ask God to fill you with hope and peace through Christ.

LESSON 8

Fear

Fear is a very powerful emotion. It's that empty feeling you get in the pit of your stomach, perhaps when you're doing something for the first time. It's the discomfort you experience that can cause you to literally shake all over.

Many of us experience fear when entering a new school, starting a new job, beginning a new relationship and so on, but each of us has had a level of fear that far surpasses these everyday fears.

That near-death experience when you just knew you were at the end. Perhaps that drug you took to appear cool, but inside you feared for your life. What if it was laced with something deadly? What if your body reacted negatively and you overdosed?

Fear is very real. It is something we all deal with on different levels. This very minute, you may be full of fear and afraid of what your life holds. Afraid of what everyone thinks of you—your family, your friends, the people you interact with each day.

How do you deal with fear? How do you muster the courage to go on with life when you're so fearful and afraid?

We may not know the answers to these questions, but God's Word has all the answers to all of life's questions.

We have referenced this passage in another lesson, but in Mark 5:25-34, we read the story of the woman who had a health issue that affected her blood. She had dealt with this problem for twelve years and had spent money trying to get medical help, but only got worse.

When she heard about Jesus and His healing power, the woman said she knew in her heart that if she could just touch Jesus's clothes, she could be healed. She saw Jesus in a crowd one day and was determined to touch Him. As soon as she touched him, she knew immediately that she had been healed.

Jesus, Who knows all things, asked who touched Him. The disciples were surprised that Jesus would ask this. After all, they were in a crowd. Anybody could have touched Him.

Because the woman knew what had happened, she was afraid. Mark 5:33 says, *But the woman fearing and trembling, knowing what was done in her, came and fell down before him, and told him all the truth.*

This lady was fearful and trembling. She was scared to death! Let's notice what this fearful lady did. First, she came to Jesus, and friend, that's exactly what you need to do when you get afraid.

It's not going to do you much good to find someone to talk to about your fears. You may share your heart and soul with someone who assures you that they will keep it secret, only to find that they betrayed your confidence. You can do just what this lady did and get to Jesus. He can help you with your fears and fill your heart with faith.

The next thing this lady did was that she fell down before Jesus. Have you humbled yourself before the Lord, kneeling helplessly before Him? I hope you have already trusted Christ to take you to heaven one day. If you haven't, make today that day.

Lastly, she told Him all the truth. That's right, she told him everything that had just happened. He already knew—He's God—but this woman told Jesus everything. You can do that, too. Whatever you're fearful and afraid of, tell Jesus all about that. He already knows, but it will help you to talk to Him in prayer and tell Him all about it. Why not do this now and tell Jesus the fears you're fighting? He is willing and able to help you!

Daily Reading

Psalm 56:3,4; Isaiah 41:13; 2 Timothy 1:7

Hebrews 13:6 – *So that we may* _____ *say, The* _____ *is my* _____ *, and I will* _____ _____ *what man shall do unto me.*

LESSON 9

Regret

I am married to an amazing husband! He works very hard at what he does, carrying on numerous items of business in a day's time. His workday frequently includes many phone calls as he collaborates with members of his team.

Whenever my husband and I are on the phone with each other, we always end the call with an "I love you." On more than one occasion, due to his busy-ness, he has been on the phone talking business with someone and has ended the call by saying, "I love you." The second this slips out, it's out there! There is immediate regret. He may grunt and groan after realizing who these words were spoken to. They may laugh about it later, but for now, there is extreme embarrassment!

That is often the way regret works. When you blow it and do something that you can't take back, it is no laughing matter. It is humiliating and shameful.

Maybe you were warned about being around certain people, but you didn't listen. Then trouble came and you regret that you didn't listen. Perhaps you were cautioned about getting involved in something, but you got involved anyway. Now you have regrets.

If only you could go back and have a re-do. Unfortunately, re-dos aren't always possible. We make our choices and then must suffer the consequences.

In Luke 22, Jesus was soon to be crucified. When He was with His disciples, He warned them of things to come. He told Peter that there would come a day when he would deny Jesus three times. Peter couldn't believe it. He even told Jesus that he would never deny Him.

By the end of the same chapter, Peter had done what he never thought he would do. He had denied the Lord three times, just as he had been told. Verse 75 tells us Peter's response to what he had done: *And he went out, and wept bitterly.*

Why did Peter weep bitterly? Because he regretted his actions against the Lord. He was so sure that he wouldn't do this traitorous deed.

We've all been there, but does that mean our lives are over? It wasn't the case with Peter. He got his heart right with the Lord and went on to be used greatly for the Lord.

Guess what? The things you've done don't mean your life is over, either. Regardless of what you've done, God can take you where you are and use your life for good and for His glory.

The devil would like to beat us down with the failures and regrets of our lives. God wants to take the things we've experienced and use them to better our own lives and to help others. That area where you messed up—thank God for what happened and ask Him to help you learn from it and use it for good.

Do you regret your wrong actions? I would hope so, but don't live in regret. Learn the lessons God has for you and then let Him use you to help someone else avoid going down the same path.

Daily Reading

Psalm 51:1-13; 1 Thessalonians 5:18

Romans 8:28 – *And we know that _____ _____ work together for _____ to them that _____ God, to them who are the called according to his _____.*

According to this verse, if we love God and do the things He wants us to do with our lives, He can work all things together for good. That's something we will never regret!

LESSON 10

How to Get and Stay on Top Side

How do you encourage yourself and get back up when you are down? We can't live on the mountaintop. You may be doing well right now. Things may be going smoothly for you now. Rest assured; it won't always be that way. There will come times when you'll be discouraged and wondering if you can make it through another day, much less the week and beyond.

There is a real example found in the Bible that tells us what to do in this scenario. In 1 Samuel 30, David had been away from home, hiding from King Saul, who was out to take his life. David had a large group of men who were with him. When they returned to their city, they were in for a surprise.

The home city, Ziklag, had been burned. All the women and children had been taken captive. Here is what verse 3 of chapter 30 says: *So David and his men came to the city, and, behold, it was burned with fire; and their wives, and their sons, and their daughters, were taken captives.*

How did David feel about all of this? The Bible says he and the people that were with him wept until they couldn't weep anymore. David was *greatly distressed* (verse 6). The men who had been with David turned against him, and now they wanted to kill him. They blamed him for what had happened.

The first part of verse 6 says, *And David was greatly distressed; for the people spake of stoning him, because the soul of all the people was grieved, every man for his sons and for his daughters.*

The story doesn't end there. David was very discouraged and not only fearing for his life at the hands of Saul; but now his own companions wanted to take his life. David did something that you and I can do that will turn situations around. The last part of verse 6 says, *but David encouraged himself in the Lord his God.*

David found encouragement for himself in the Lord. When your encouragement is left up to you, your only hope is to go to the Lord. People won't always be able to encourage you. Many times, people will kick you when you are down. You don't have to stay down—encourage yourself in the Lord!

You can open the pages of God's Word and find help and hope. This is something you need to learn well, because there will be many times when this is all you may have to which to cling. God can use His Word to lift you out of your despair and raise you up from the depths of discouragement.

You can find so much encouragement in the book of Psalms. Did you know that it was David who God used to write much of the Psalms? Yes, this same man who often faced discouragement was used by God to help countless people find encouragement in their times of despair.

Don't wait for someone to come along and pat you on the back and tell you everything will be okay. They may never show up, but God will! Open His Word and read it until God lifts you up. Anytime you feel yourself sinking down, run to Jesus. Open your

Bible and begin reading. You will be amazed at what this will do to get you on top side again.

Daily Reading

1 Samuel 30:1-6

Psalm 27:14 – _____ on the Lord: be of _____, and he shall _____ thine _____: wait, I say, on the _____.

LESSON 11

Maximizing Your Time (Making Your Days Count)

There are times when we get in a slump. We are not motivated to do anything, even the things that are necessary for us to do.

You may be in a position where you feel your life is at a standstill, going nowhere fast. This is not a position you want to remain in.

If you have not already done so, you need to decide each day to improve yourself. There may be some factors present in your life that you can't change, but you can work on making even small changes in your life.

Some find it very hard to get motivated when they are down. Many in this position will just simply sleep the day away. This will only cause you to be even more down on yourself. Don't let yourself be one of those individuals. You need to maximize the opportunities that you have.

What exactly can you do? Start by building your relationship with the Lord. You can set all sorts of dreams and goals, and you should; but first, focus on what is most important. Make sure you have accepted Christ and know that you have a home in heaven one day.

If you're sure of your eternal home, put the Lord first in your daily life. When you wake up in the morning, stop and thank God for the new day. You can begin your day with God, seeking wisdom from His Word. Matthew 6:33 says, *But seek ye first the kingdom of God, and his righteousness; and all these things shall be added unto you.*

The verses in this chapter are referring to cares of this life: what we will eat and drink, what clothes we will wear, and so on. When we put God first in our lives and seek Him, He promises to take care of all our needs.

Have a daily time where you care for your health. Maybe this is walking or doing some sort of cardio exercises. You only get one body. Do your best to properly care for it.

You may have done some harmful things to your body such as drug or alcohol use. Realize that these things are not going to make your life better. They are only temporary "fixes," though they only leave your life even more broken.

Spend some time working on things that can benefit you. What are your talents and abilities? What are you good at? You can lay out a plan to pursue some of these things. Get some books or information on these subjects and be a continuous learner.

Having a daily routine can be a game changer in your life. It will cause your life to be more scheduled and will allow you to have a feeling of accomplishment each day. You should give your all to get a hard routine established as quickly as possible and stick with it. You can't change your history, but your future can be bright and full of promise.

Proverbs 29:18 says this: *Where there is no vision, the people perish: but he that keepeth the law, happy is he.* Do you have a vision of what your future will be like? If you were to sit down and dream about how your ideal life would be, what would that look like for you?

Get a vision of what your life can be. Those with no vision die. This doesn't have to be you. Pray and ask God what He wants from your life. Write down the things He brings to your mind, including how you can use the lessons you're learning right now through your dark hour to help others. When you have free time, dream about these ideas and implant them deep in your heart. There is no limit as to what God can do with your life!

Daily Reading

James 4:14; Ephesians 5:16; Colossians 4:5

The last two verses mention "redeeming the time." The word redeem means "to gain or regain possession of." You may have some wasted years in your history. Redeem the time and gain it back by using the time you have now for God and good.

Write out Matthew 6:33 in the space provided.

LESSON 12

Overcoming Shame and Guilt

Often when you find yourself in a place where you've let others down and you've disappointed your loved ones, you can struggle with the guilt of your actions. This is okay initially to an extent because it allows you to own up to what you've done and even lead you to make things right.

There are many who commit heinous crimes and have no remorse at all. This attitude is totally wrong! We all must admit our wrongdoings, but once we have, we must move forward. God will forgive all our sins if we ask Him.

Let's suppose you had a problem with drugs. Maybe your family had tried to get help for you, but things didn't go well. You relapsed on more than one occasion. Understanding the struggles that come with addiction, your family chose to forgive you and give you yet another chance.

Yet, no matter how hard you tried, you couldn't seem to forgive yourself. You beat yourself up relentlessly. You told yourself so many lies:

- "I'll never get away from this life of addiction."
- "Why keep trying? I'm just going to mess up again."
- "Everyone else has given up on me, so there's no point in trying anyway."
- "This is just too hard to overcome."

These are all lies that the devil wants to feed you and get you to embrace.

If you have accepted Christ, you can go to Him at any time with any sin you have committed. We're all guilty of some awful things. Imagine the things you've done that no one even knows about. Yet God willingly forgives those who come to Him for forgiveness.

If you've confessed your sins to the Lord, you must accept His forgiveness. The devil will bring up your faults over and over, but you must rest in the fact that those sins are gone. You don't have to be held captive to guilt. You need to claim the forgiveness that's been given to you.

Consider this verse from 1 John 1:9: *If we confess our sins, he is faithful and just to forgive us our sins and to cleanse us from all unrighteousness.* What an amazing verse! This verse assures us that God forgives and cleanses our sins when we confess them to him.

When Satan comes to remind you of what you've done—and he will—you have to remind him of what God says. This is something you will have to do repeatedly because the devil has a way of making you feel guilty about your past sins. Claim the forgiveness that's been offered to you.

LESSON 12

Overcoming Shame and Guilt

Often when you find yourself in a place where you've let others down and you've disappointed your loved ones, you can struggle with the guilt of your actions. This is okay initially to an extent because it allows you to own up to what you've done and even lead you to make things right.

There are many who commit heinous crimes and have no remorse at all. This attitude is totally wrong! We all must admit our wrongdoings, but once we have, we must move forward. God will forgive all our sins if we ask Him.

Let's suppose you had a problem with drugs. Maybe your family had tried to get help for you, but things didn't go well. You relapsed on more than one occasion. Understanding the struggles that come with addiction, your family chose to forgive you and give you yet another chance.

Yet, no matter how hard you tried, you couldn't seem to forgive yourself. You beat yourself up relentlessly. You told yourself so many lies:

- "I'll never get away from this life of addiction."
- "Why keep trying? I'm just going to mess up again."
- "Everyone else has given up on me, so there's no point in trying anyway."
- "This is just too hard to overcome."

These are all lies that the devil wants to feed you and get you to embrace.

If you have accepted Christ, you can go to Him at any time with any sin you have committed. We're all guilty of some awful things. Imagine the things you've done that no one even knows about. Yet God willingly forgives those who come to Him for forgiveness.

If you've confessed your sins to the Lord, you must accept His forgiveness. The devil will bring up your faults over and over, but you must rest in the fact that those sins are gone. You don't have to be held captive to guilt. You need to claim the forgiveness that's been given to you.

Consider this verse from 1 John 1:9: *If we confess our sins, he is faithful and just to forgive us our sins and to cleanse us from all unrighteousness.* What an amazing verse! This verse assures us that God forgives and cleanses our sins when we confess them to him.

When Satan comes to remind you of what you've done—and he will—you have to remind him of what God says. This is something you will have to do repeatedly because the devil has a way of making you feel guilty about your past sins. Claim the forgiveness that's been offered to you.

Daily Reading

Psalm 103:1-14

According to verse 12 in this passage, what does God do with our sins (iniquities)?

LESSON 13

Dealing With Pride

There are a lot of places you can go and meet people who are very proud. You can go to a college campus or university and find people who are proud of their knowledge. Drive through a wealthy neighborhood and you will find many who are proud of their wealth. Attend a sporting event and you are bound to find athletes who are proud of their physical abilities.

Did you know that in the Bible, there is nothing good spoken about pride? Not one verse mentions pride as a good thing, yet we hear of and see pride all around us every day.

Wherever you go, there is pride. Some are proud of the things they have done, even though they are bad things. Others have feelings of pride that cause them to think they are better than others.

Looking at God's Word gives us some insight on pride and will direct us to have the right perspective on this subject.

In 2 Corinthians 10:12, the Bible says, *For we dare not make ourselves of the number, or compare ourselves with some that commend themselves: but they measuring themselves by themselves, and comparing themselves among themselves, are not wise.*

According to this verse, there were some people who were commending themselves. In other words, they felt worthy of praise and worthy of being noticed. God says we dare not do this!

Basically, these people compare themselves with others. The Bible says it is not wise to do this.

We can look good when we find someone else who we think is worse off than us, but what about when we line up our lives with the Lord? This can put us in our places very quickly!

Pride is a dangerous thing. Notice what Proverbs 16:18 says: *Pride goeth before destruction, and an haughty spirit before a fall.* That person who is puffed up with pride will soon face destruction. He is bound to experience a fall.

Proverbs 11:2 says, *When pride cometh, then cometh shame: but with the lowly is wisdom.* Shame is another fruit of pride. It is the humble person who exercises wisdom.

Guard your heart against pride. Nothing good can come from it, but God can bless one who exercises humility.

Daily Reading
Luke 18:9-14

Proverbs 29:23 – *A man's _____ shall bring him _____: but _____ shall uphold the _____ in spirit.*

LESSON 14

Helplessness

What do you do when there is absolutely nothing you can do? You are certain to face situations that leave you feeling helpless. There are times when you may be very dependent on others even for everyday necessities.

Feeling helpless can cause you to experience emotions of inadequacy. You can be very down on yourself and even feel like a failure.

Psalm 72:12 says, *For he shall deliver the needy when he crieth; the poor also, and him that hath no helper.* This is a promise you can cling to. God promises to deliver the needy, the poor, and those that have no helper. Does this describe you? You can lean on the Lord, asking for His help in your time of need.

Any good mother loves hers children and wants the best for them, but do you know that God loves the kids even more than mothers do? There are many times when you will be helpless as it relates to your children, especially when they are adults. They may be dealing with things they don't want you involved in. Ask God for His help with your children.

One of the most powerful things you can do for your kids is to pray for them. Pray for their safety and protection. Pray for them to be kept from evil. There are many who would seek to harm children and do evil things to them and with them. Pray for your children like you've never prayed before. You can spend time worrying about them, but what good will that do? Pray for them!

I've heard of many stories about praying mothers. Even in her elderly years, my mother could be found on her knees every morning praying for each of her children. Your prayers could literally save your child's life. I've said this myself and heard many others say it in situations that seem hopeless: "All we can do is pray." All we can do? That's a slap in the face of God! That is one of our most powerful weapons. Use it to protect your children.

Daily Reading

Mark 10:13-16

Write out the following verse and do your best to live by it.

1 Thessalonians 5:17

LESSON 15

Dealing with Being Judged

Think of the feeling you get when you stand before a judge in a courtroom. Most people get very anxious and uptight. This person holds your future in their hands. It can be a very scary situation.

Have you ever been in a situation where you felt as if you were being judged by someone who didn't even know you, much less know what you've been through? We've all been there, but we've also been on the flip side where we've been the ones guilty of casting judgment.

When you deal with people making judgment calls about your life, it can cause great insecurity. You can build up an entire scenario in your mind that can be totally false. This is very damaging mentally.

People love jumping to conclusions without having all the facts. It is a difficult thing to have people judge you without knowing all the facts of your situation. How do you deal with this?

We can't allow ourselves to be consumed with what people think about us or what we "think" they think about us. Often when we create scenarios mentally, it is as if we think we are mind readers, knowing the thoughts that must be going through another person's mind. Many times, when we think people are judging us, they are too busy hoping we are not judging them.

I've personally had to confess my shortcomings in this area many times. I may make a judgment call and end up being totally wrong in my presumptions.

Do you know that God is the Judge of all the earth (Genesis 18:25)? One day, we will all stand before Him. His judgment on our lives should be feared far more than any earthly judge or person who may try to judge our lives.

We need to be concerned with what God thinks about our actions. If we focused our energy on this and on making sure we are pleasing God, it would matter very little to us what others may think of us.

Consider the following verse in Galatians 1:10: *For do I now persuade men, or God? or do I seek to please men? for if I yet pleased men, I should not be the servant of Christ.* People can always find fault with you. Don't look to be a people-pleaser. Spend your energies pleasing the One who truly matters.

It has been said that the greatest prison people live in is the fear of what other people think. How true is that statement!

Learn the habit of giving people grace rather than casting judgment and assuming you know all the facts. Maybe, just maybe, you don't know the whole story. One day you will want someone to be gracious to you. Offer that same grace to others.

Here is a thought to ponder: Instead of putting others in their place, put yourself in their place. If you can begin practicing this with others, you will find that you will reap what you sow and be given the same grace you've given to others.

Daily Reading
Luke 18:9-14

Psalm 19:14 – *Let the _____ of my _____, and the _____ of my _____, be acceptable in _____ _____, O Lord, my _____, and my redeemer.*

LESSON 16

Are You Overwhelmed?

We are all familiar with Murphy's law which says, "Anything that can go wrong will go wrong." There are times when it seems we just can't catch a break. Life can be overwhelming to the point where we just don't know how we can bear any more. Times like these can lead us to believe we just can't go on.

How do you keep going when everything in you is telling you to just quit and give up? There are many examples in the Bible of people who at some point in their lives got overwhelmed. They were submerged by their circumstances. Yet there are many examples of those who were not resigned to staying in the state of being overwhelmed.

There are some specific instructions given in God's Word about what to do when we get overwhelmed. Psalm 61:2 says, *From the end of the earth will I cry unto thee, when my heart is overwhelmed: lead me to the rock that is higher than I.*

Verses 1 and 2 of this same chapter mention that David was crying out to God. Being overwhelmed can certainly bring us to tears. We can be in a rough situation that causes us to break down and cry.

We can cry tears of frustration, tears of anger, tears of sorrow, and so forth. Did you know that you can cry out to God and tell Him all that is on your heart? Not only that, but He knows and understands your heartache. Sometimes you can cry to others and wonder if they even care what you are going through. You won't find that to be the case with God. He cares!

You may share your problems with those around you, only to find that they have betrayed your confidence and shared your trouble with others. The safest place for you to go when you get overwhelmed is to the arms of Jesus. Cry to Him and let Him wrap you in His arms of love and assure you that He is with you.

How comforting it is when you get overwhelmed to have someone place their arms around you and tell you they love you. This may not solve the problems, but it surely does give comfort. God will give you comfort like no other when you run and cry to Him.

You may have memories of one of your own children getting badly hurt and coming to you with tears streaming down their face. A loving mother will comfort the child and help them with whatever hurt they may be experiencing. God loves you far more than you can ever love anyone. Pour out your heart to Him.

1 Peter 5:7 says, *Casting all your care upon him; for he careth for you.* What cares do you have today? You can cast them all on the Lord. Why? Because He cares for you!

Consider the words to the chorus of this hymn written by Frank E. Graeff:

Oh, yes, He cares, I know He cares,
His heart is touched with my grief;
When the days are weary, the long nights dreary,
I know my Savior cares.

No one will ever care for you like Jesus does. He is the strong Rock that you need to stand firm on for support when life overwhelms you.

Daily Reading

Matthew 7:24-25; Psalm 31:3; Psalm 62:7

Write out Psalm 94:22 in the space below.

LESSON 17

Getting the Load Off Your Back

~~~

You've heard the expression, "Take a load off." This expression is typically used by someone who is encouraging you to relax. Maybe they noticed your tired look or that you looked burdened down. They're inviting you to a time of relaxation.

The Lord also makes us an offer to ease our burden and give us rest. Here's what He says in Matthew 11:28-30: *Come unto me, all ye that labour and are heavy laden, and I will give you rest. Take my yoke upon you, and learn of me; for I am meek and lowly in heart: and ye shall find rest unto your souls. For my yoke is easy, and my burden is light.*

What an offer! Just by coming to the Lord with my burdens, He will give me rest. Life can weigh you down with all its burdens and cares. You can be working your hardest to deal with all that comes your way and still feel as if you're spinning your wheels and going nowhere.

Jesus invites you to come to Him. Bring your burdens and your problems and give them to Jesus. In the Bible, a "yoke" is a harness used by oxen and other animals to ease the work of hauling a load. Jesus tells us to take His yoke and learn of Him. You can get in the yoke with Jesus. You're right beside Him, but He is the One bearing the load. He says His yoke is easy.

I can journey through life struggling to bear my load or I can get beside Jesus and let Him lighten my load. Our lives will always be burdensome when we are focused on ourselves and our problems.

When was the last time you did something for someone else? One of the best things you can do to ease your burdens is to think of others and how you can be a help to them. This is the way Jesus lived, always thinking of others: who He could heal, who He could feed, whose life He could touch.

Living your life after His example or taking His burden (caring for others) will cause you to forget about your own troubles. You will find rest as Jesus then cares for your load.

Many times, I've been focused on my own problems, and then had the opportunity to do something for someone who could do nothing in return for me. I am always encouraged and find my own burden is lifted.

Remember the good feeling you got inside when you helped that elderly person at the grocery store, that stranger you helped when they dropped something in the store, that person you noticed who was discouraged to whom you offered encouragement? When you stepped in and tried to help someone else, it never fails that you forget about your own problems.

We can live our lives for others and find our own burdens aren't so heavy. The Lord will hold us up if we will just give our burdens to Him.

Daily Reading

Psalm 55:22; Galatians 6:2; 1 Peter 5:7

Write out one of the above verses that will remind you to take your burdens to the Lord and focus on helping others.

LESSON 18

Attacking Panic Before It Attacks You

A panic attack is defined as a sudden episode of intense fear that triggers severe physical reactions when there is no real danger or apparent cause. They are caused by extreme anxiety. Can these be avoided and if so, how?

Our minds are often plagued by "what ifs" and situations that cause us to worry and fret. We can worry so much to the point where it affects our bodies. How can we stop this cycle and prevent this from happening?

The Bible has the answer to any problem we may face in this life. Luke 10:38-42 tells the story of two sisters. One of the two sisters (Martha) seemed to be very busy serving, for Jesus had come to their home for a visit. The other sister (Mary) was sitting at Jesus's feet, listening to him as He spoke.

Martha was getting upset. Here she was doing all she could to serve, and Mary was just sitting there doing nothing to help. Martha even got so bold that she asked Jesus if He even cared that she had been left to do all the work by herself. She must have been fuming inside as she rushed around to care for their guest while Mary did nothing to help her out.

Rather than Jesus calling Mary out, He told Martha that she was too full of care and that she was troubled about many things. Jesus looked beyond what seemed to be the obvious issue and looked at the heart of the matter. He knew that Martha had a lot on her plate. She was very likely consumed with worry, not just about serving Jesus and making sure everything was good, but she was troubled about many things.

Isn't it easy to have our minds overrun with worry? This was certainly true for Martha, and we can all relate to how worry can overtake us. Jesus responded to Martha by telling her that only one thing was needful—taking time to be with Jesus.

Sometimes we can get so busy doing other things that we forget about what's most important—our relationship with Jesus. If Martha was already troubled about many things when Jesus showed up, she could have taken all the things that were causing her to be anxious to Jesus and let Him help her deal with them.

When Jesus is present in your life, there is no need to be worried and fearful about anything. Think of how much boldness a fearful child has when there is an adult present to guide them through that fear. The dark and scary room is not so intimidating anymore when there is a mother present holding the child's hand.

When you begin to sense the emotions of fear and anxiety, get in the presence of your heavenly Father immediately for victory over your issues. To let these emotions run free in your mind means you are allowing them to grow and multiply, and they will soon overpower you.

You can attack your panic before it attacks you. The Lord can give you peace and calmness when circumstances threaten to overwhelm you with fear. God doesn't want your heart to be full of worry and care. Why worry when you can pray? Pray more and you will worry less.

Daily Reading

Philippians 4:6-8; 1 Peter 5:7; Luke 24:38; John 14:1

John 14:27 – _____ I leave with you, my _____ I give unto you: not as the _____ giveth, give I unto you. Let not your _____ be _____, neither let it be _____.

LESSON 19

The God of Hope

There are some people who have specialties in certain fields and that is the area in which they excel. They may even be considered an expert in their trade. There are others who seem to be talented in many different areas. We might call this person a jack of all trades.

God is infinite in His power. The Bible says in Jeremiah 32:17 that there is nothing too hard for Him. He has many titles, but there is one that we will emphasize for this lesson.

Romans 15:13 says, *Now the God of hope fill you with all joy and peace in believing, that ye may abound in hope, through the power of the Holy Ghost.*

Notice in this verse that God is called the God of _____. What an incredible title! That means that all hope is rooted in Him. This tells us that when we are lacking hope or even at the point of hopelessness, He is the One we should be seeking if we want to find hope.

Often people turn to so many other people and things to find hope. You may have placed your hope in people, only to have lost hope in them. Someone may have placed their hope in you, and unfortunately, you may have failed them. True hope is rooted in Christ.

Sometimes our hopes get delayed. We may have our minds set upon something taking place at a certain time. When it doesn't happen, we may lose our hope. Proverbs 13:12 says, *Hope deferred maketh the heart sick: but when the desire cometh, it is a tree of life.* Losing hope can give us a sick feeling inside. Make sure your hope is in the Lord and not in things and people who can disappoint you.

Our hope needs to be anchored in God. We have the promises of His Word that are true and unfailing. The Bible says in Psalm 130:5, *I wait for the LORD, my soul doth wait, and in his word do I hope.* We must place our hope in the eternal Word of God.

This verse tells us that God wants us to not only realize that He is our hope, but He wants us to abound in hope. The word abound means "to be present in large numbers or in great quantity." God doesn't just want us to have hope, but He wants us to abound in hope.

Daily Reading

Psalm 31:24; Psalm 33:18; Psalm 38:15; Psalm 78:7

What word is the theme of each of these verses? _____

Write out the verse from these passages that touched your heart the most.

LESSON 20

Emotional Roller Coasters

Are you a roller coaster enthusiast? Do you enjoy the thrill of getting your blood flowing from the excitement and hype of a good roller coaster? For some, roller coasters give an exhilarating rush of adrenaline in just a very short amount of time.

Those who enjoy roller coasters love the feeling of the unknown that they give. You reach the top and just about the time you catch your breath, you plunge to the bottom at an intensely high rate of speed.

Then there are others who may have gotten on the ride due to some coaxing by someone who encouraged or even dared them to get on. The ups and downs, loops and twists may be fun for some while others vow to never ride again.

What about when your life is like a roller coaster? You get excited about the good times when life is good and then you get down in the dumps when life takes a turn, threatening to turn you upside down. You can be flying high one day and the next be in the depths of despair.

How can you live a life of stability no matter what life throws at you? There is nothing worse than being around someone who is unpredictable in their mood. They are good when things are good, but a pain to be around when things are bad.

All of us are going to have good and bad days, but we don't have to wear our emotions on our sleeves. Our lives don't have to be lived in such a way that people don't know how to approach us, for fear that we may be in a mood that can cause us to be undesirable to be around.

Proverbs 16:32 says, *He that is slow to anger is better than the mighty; and he that ruleth his spirit than he that taketh a city.* Do you rule your spirit (your mood or temper), or does your spirit rule you? A person who is slow to anger is stronger than a mighty person. When you control your spirit, it is a powerful thing.

Proverbs 17:27 says, *He that hath knowledge spareth his words: and a man of understanding is of an excellent spirit.* Often people let their emotions determine their temperament. If they are upset, they may spew out foul and hurtful words to those who just happen to be in the line of fire. We need to be careful with our words and strive to have an excellent spirit.

How often does a child have to pay for the parent flying off the handle? What did they do to deserve your wrath? You need to control your emotions and ask the Lord for wisdom to handle situations that would normally cause you to react in ways that are not good.

One very quick way to lift your spirits is to sit down and write down all your blessings. You will find that there is always something to be thankful for and you will discover that things are not as bad as you may think.

Consider these words from 1 Corinthians 6:20: *For ye are bought with a price: therefore glorify God in your body, and in your spirit, which are God's.* Christ has purchased our salvation. If you have accepted Him, your body and your spirit need to glorify Him.

The Issues of Life

If you don't like the ups and downs of living on an emotional roller coaster, allow the Lord to help you have a spirit that is pleasing to Him.

Daily Reading

Galatians 5:22-23; 1 Timothy 4:12; 1 Thessalonians 5:18

Proverbs 3:5-6 – _____ in the _____ with all thine _____; And _____ not unto thine own _____. In _____ thy _____ acknowledge _____, and he shall _____ thy _____.

LESSON 21

Gossip

Have you ever been caught off guard and hit by someone by surprise? Maybe you were in your own little world when someone either accidentally or intentionally hit you. It can be jarring, as it comes without warning, and you have no time to brace yourself.

What about when someone purposely hurts you, not physically, but verbally? Physical hurts are bad enough, but just as hurtful are words spoken about us. These harmful words have a way of making their way back to us, and the pain is often felt long after we hear the words.

Here is what the Bible has to say about our tongues: *But the tongue can no man tame; it is an unruly evil, full of deadly poison* (James 3:8).

The Bible says that our tongues can't be tamed. They are an unruly evil and they are full of deadly poison. What does poison do? It is defined by Webster's Dictionary as "a substance that through its chemical action usually kills, injures, or impairs an organism." This is the kind of power our tongues have.

You wouldn't drink something if you knew it contained poison, yet the Bible says our tongues are full of deadly poison. Our words not only injure, but also kill.

Think of a wild beast, maybe a tiger. Would you get within petting distance if you were told that the tiger was tame? Not likely to happen! Why? Because this is a wild animal and regardless of how much training it has been through, it is not a tamed animal.

The same is true of our tongues. Because the tongue can't be tamed, we have no reason to trust it. How many times have we had the strong urge inside to tell someone something we knew about someone else? There is almost an irresistible urge inside just to tell someone! We hold back for as long as we can, and then, when we can no longer resist, out it comes.

We don't mind joining in and sharing gossip, but if we reap what we sow, we have to remember that at some point, we will be the object of gossip. This should give us great pause with what we say and what we hear.

Psalm 19:14 says, *Let the words of my mouth, and the meditation of my heart, be acceptable in thy sight, O LORD, my strength, and my redeemer.* We need to make sure that our words and the thoughts of our hearts are acceptable in the Lord's sight. He has the highest standard of all. I may think my words are fine, but what does God think?

Consider Psalm 141:3: *Set a watch, O LORD, before my mouth; keep the door of my lips.* How careful we will be when we allow the Lord to watch over our mouths and to guard our lips!

Not only should you not gossip, but you also need to be sure not to listen to gossip. Maybe you are careful not to gossip, but if you listen to gossip about others, that is equally wrong.

You are telling a lot about yourself when you listen to gossip. Proverbs 17:4 says, *A wicked doer giveth heed to false lips; and a liar giveth ear to a naughty tongue.* God calls the one who listens to false lips "wicked," and the one who listens to a naughty tongue "a liar." If you don't want to be considered wicked or a liar, make sure that the words you listen to are right words.

Daily Reading

Proverbs 18:8, 20:19, 26:22

What do you notice about Proverbs 18:8 and Proverbs 26:22?

Anything God mentions is important, but if He mentions the same things more than once, we need to really make sure we are listening to what He says.

LESSON 22

When Life Isn't Fair (Dealing with Injustices)

How many times have you heard the phrase, "That's not fair!" Not only have you heard it dozens of times, but how often have you been the one talking about how unfair a situation is?

You have also heard it said that life is not fair. If you are a parent, this is the typical response to your child when you hear them talk about how unfair something is. The fact is, we will face many injustices in this life.

How do you handle situations when you are on the receiving end of injustices? Do you fly off the handle and let everyone around you endure your wrath? Does it push you to do things you will later regret?

Since injustices are a regular part of life, we need to know how to handle ourselves when things don't go our way. We can't control what other people do to us, but we can control our responses to them.

Let's look at the example of Joseph in the Bible. Joseph experienced injustices from a very young age. He had ten brothers who hated him and could not speak peaceably to him. They hated him so much that they wanted to kill him.

One day they planned to kill him and cast him into a pit. One brother discouraged them from killing him and told them to just cast him into a pit.

After they put him in a pit, merchants came by, drew him out of the pit, and sold him into Egypt to be a slave. Even in this predicament, Joseph had God's favor upon his life. The Bible says several times that God was with him. As a servant, everything he did was well pleasing to his master, so much so that he was promoted and made overseer.

Along came his master's wife. She tried to convince Joseph to sleep with her, but he refused. She kept after him until one day, she grabbed his garment. Joseph ran away, leaving his garment in her hands. She then lied about him and told Joseph's master that he tried to rape her. This earned him a trip to prison for something he did not do.

We find another example of injustice in Joseph's life when he helped some men who were in prison. After helping them, Joseph asked them not to forget him so that he could be brought out of prison. He was forgotten for quite some time by someone he helped. Life surely didn't seem fair at that point in his life.

Joseph was later called upon to help Pharaoh and because of this, he was delivered from prison. God prospered his life even through all that he endured.

Here is the statement Joseph made in Genesis 50:20: *But as for you, ye thought evil against me; but God meant it unto good, to bring to pass, as it is this day, to save much people alive.*

Joseph had endured a lot of injustices, but his perspective was that God had a purpose in all of it. He didn't live his life as if he were a victim of circumstances. He allowed God to use even the "bad" things that happened to further His cause.

The wrongs that you endure, you can be thankful for them. The Bible tells us in 1 Thessalonians 5:18, *In every thing give thanks: for this is the will of God in Christ Jesus concerning you.* "Every thing" is not just good things, but bad things as well.

This is not always an easy thing to do, but giving thanks will cause you to avoid having the victim mentality. It will also guard your heart from developing bitterness inside. God can take the unfair things you have experienced and use them in your life to enable you to help others.

Consider all the injustices Christ endured for us. Remember, He was perfect and never sinned, yet He willingly suffered for our sins. We are to follow the example He has set for us.

Daily Reading
1 Peter 2:21-25; Hebrews 12:2-3

1 Peter 3:18 – *For _____ also hath once _____ for sins, the _____ for the_____, that he might _____ us to God, being put to _____ in the flesh, but quickened by the _____:*

LESSON 23

Dealing with Grief

Often people find out terrible news about loved ones. They may have family members who are sick, who have life-threatening news, or worse yet, who have died. This can be extremely difficult and can cause us to experience helplessness and deep sorrow.

How would you handle it if you were in a situation similar to this? If you have a loved one who has been given only a small window of time left on earth, you may grieve and be heavy hearted. In some instances, you may be distant and unable to be present with the loved one.

Not being able to be there could easily cause you to feel badly. This in turn causes guilt and your mind goes in a downward spiral.

So how do you process the grief when you are unable to be with family in such a time of sadness?

The ultimate hardship is the loss of a family member. If our loved one had accepted Christ, it gives hope to know that we will one day see them again. That is why it is so important to share Christ with others. Many times, when people die, the statement is made, "Rest in peace." We are saddened by hearing of someone's death, but we can't automatically assume the person knew the Lord. We need to do all we can to make sure our friends and family are saved.

When dealing with grief, you can often find comfort in being close to those you love. When that is not possible, you can support your family through prayer. The Lord is able to comfort like no other can.

Do you know that the Word of God can comfort your heart? Listen to these words from Romans 15:4: *For whatsoever things were written aforetime were written for our learning, that we through patience and comfort of the scriptures might have hope.* Notice the phrase, "comfort of the scriptures." God can use His Word to give you comfort in your time of grief. Use this healing balm and you will find comfort for your heart.

There are many things that can cause us grief. When someone we love is hurting, we hurt right along with them. This grief can take place right inside your home. You may grieve over a child making poor decisions that will bring them harm. Your grief may be in the form of a bad decision you make.

Regardless of the source of your grief, take these issues to God in prayer. Don't try to carry the load yourself. Allow the Lord to give you strength to endure the hardship and to enable you to make it through. We will all go through storms, but remember, it won't rain forever. This, too, shall pass!

Daily Reading

Matthew 5:4; 2 Corinthians 1:3-4; 2 Corinthians 7:6

In 2 Corinthians 1:3, God is called the _____ of all _____.

2 Corinthians 7:6 says that God _____ those that are _____ _____.

LESSON 24

What to Do When Your Life Has No Purpose

Have you ever looked at your life and said, "I have no idea why I'm here on this earth." Perhaps at one time, your life was on target for success. Many young people often begin early in life talking about what they want to become when they grow up, but by the time they should be working toward their life purpose, that dream has grown fuzzy.

So exactly why are you here? What is the meaning of your life? Is it to be whatever you choose to be? To be successful? To be happy? Your reply may be, "I don't even know."

If this is you, don't be content with not being able to give a good answer to this question. As always, the Bible has the answer to every one of life's questions.

James 4:14 says, *Whereas ye know not what shall be on the morrow. For what is your life? It is even a vapour, that appeareth for a little time, and then vanisheth away.* To understand your life, it is important to remember how short it is. You are not promised tomorrow. Your time on this earth is short and you need to make it count.

There are things you can do with your life that can shorten it. Many verses in the Bible explain how unwise choices can cause your life to be shortened. Yet there are many principles you can follow that will lengthen your days.

Proverbs 3:1-2 says, *My son, forget not my law; but let thine heart keep my commandments: For length of days, and long life, and peace, shall they add to thee.* This passage explains how a son who keeps his father's commandment can have length of days, long life, and peace. These are fruits of an obedient life.

Getting wisdom is another way to enjoy the blessing of a fruitful life. Proverbs 9:11 says, *For by me thy days shall be multiplied, and the years of thy life shall be increased.* The "me" in this verse is referring to wisdom. When you ask God for wisdom for your life, He will give it to you and help you make wise decisions that can multiply your days and increase your years.

What does God want with your life? Matthew 10:39 tells us, *He that findeth his life shall lose it: and he that loseth his life for my sake shall find it.* Many in this world today seek to find their own life's purpose. This is the mentality that, "It's my life and I can do what I want with it."

For the believer, you will never "find" your life by doing your own thing and going about life your own way. Your life is to be lived for God and others. This is the key to having a happy, blessed life. Living life apart from God's pattern will only cause you discontentment and unhappiness.

Consider what 1 Corinthians 6:20 says: *For ye are bought with a price: therefore glorify God in your body, and in your spirit, which are God's.* Your life has been purchased by the blood of Christ. Verse 19 of this same chapter tells us, *ye are not your own.*

God has given every one of us gifts and abilities. No two people have the same gifts. There are gifts you have that are diverse from those around you, but each of our gifts are needed. That is the beauty of the body of Christ. We all have different purposes, but they all work together for the good of the body.

Rather than asking, "What do I want to do with my life," why not ask God what He wants to do with your life? Allow God to have His way in your life and live your life with no regrets.

Daily Reading

Acts 9:6

This verse asks a question that we all should ask the Lord. Write the question below and why not take time to ask the Lord this same question for your life.

John 10:10

The _____ cometh not, but for to _____, and to _____, and to _____: I am come that they might have _____, and that they might have it more _____.

According to this verse, God wants us to have an _____ life.

Matthew 6:33 – *But seek ye _____ the kingdom of _____, and his _____; and all these _____ shall be added unto you.*

When we seek the Lord and what He wants for us, He will provide for us all the things that we get so caught up with in this life.

LESSON 25

Resisting Temptation

Have you ever made up your mind that you were not going to do something that was bad for you? It may be something as simple as a diet that says you can't have sweets. Now, suddenly, all you can think about is having something sweet. It is constantly on your mind, even more so than before you started your diet.

How do you resist temptations that carry far greater consequences than giving in to a forbidden food? What if the temptation is over something that can cause harm to yourself and others?

Often when a person gets involved in a destructive lifestyle, along with it comes certain habits that are just as harmful. You now must cover your wrongdoing so no one will find out, and so the lying game begins.

One of the worst things about the habit of lying is that you must keep track of your lies and to whom you told them. You must have a perfect track history with lying for your deception to be successful. It's a much easier thing to simply tell the truth.

Each of us have different areas where we may be tempted to do wrong. What will you do when you're faced with the temptation to do wrong?

The Bible gives us many ways to help us deal with temptation. Jesus was also tempted to do wrong. The devil tried to tempt Him just as he tries to tempt us. We can look at the example of Christ and see what we're to do when temptations come.

In Matthew 4, the devil came to Jesus three times trying to get Him to do wrong. How did Jesus respond? He used the Word of God. For each temptation, Jesus quoted the Word.

When the devil comes to tempt you, remember that he will not just try one time to get you to give in. He will keep coming back again and again, hoping you will give in to the temptation. You must stand fast on God's Word.

Whatever your sin is that you struggle with the most, get some verses from the Bible that will remind you of what the Bible says about it. If you are tempted by drugs or alcohol, find verses that will help you resist the devil.

You are not alone in dealing with temptations. The Bible tells us in 1 Corinthians 10:13 that temptations are common things for all of us: *There hath no temptation taken you but such as is common to man: but God is faithful, who will not suffer you to be tempted above that ye are able; but will with the temptation also make a way to escape, that ye may be able to bear it.* For every temptation you face, God provides a way of escape for you. Look for the way of escape when you are faced with temptation.

You can pray that you will not enter into temptation. Mark 14:38 says, *Watch ye and pray, lest ye enter into temptation. The spirit truly is ready, but the flesh is weak.* Be on the lookout for things that could cause temptation and avoid them. Pray and ask God to help you not to enter into temptation.

This verse is also a good reminder that you are not as strong as you think. You can have good intentions, but your flesh is weak.

Stay away from people and places that you know will be sources of temptation for you. You are not strong enough to resist temptations when in bad situations. Don't let the devil convince you that you can handle temptation and then find out later that you really couldn't.

Notice the cycle and progression of sin. James 1:14-15 says, *But every man is tempted, when he is drawn away of his own lust, and enticed. Then when lust hath conceived, it bringeth forth sin: and sin, when it is finished, bringeth forth death.* It starts with temptation. Our lusts cause us to be drawn and enticed to do sinful things.

These lustful feelings lead to sin. When our sin has completed its cycle, it ends in death. We must earnestly pray that the Lord will keep us from even being tempted by the things that are not good.

Using these ideas can help you to deal with temptation when it comes your way. Don't just give in and suffer the consequences. Don't yield to temptation!

Daily Reading

Matthew 4:1-10; Galatians 5:16-17

James 4:7 – _____ *yourselves therefore to* _____. *Resist the* _____, *and he will* _____ *from you.*

When we yield to God and do what He wants us to do, what will the devil's response be?

LESSON 26

Dealing with Mental Trauma from Past Experiences

Have you ever had something that you just couldn't seem to get off your mind? This may be a thought or idea that your mind won't let go of. It could even be something you've experienced that plagues you day in and out. It's as if someone has pressed the repeat button of this image in your mind.

Things like this can be a source of mental torment. How do you stop the anguish of mind?

You may deal with these images due to something you endured: physical, mental, or emotional abuse. Instead of images, it may be words that haunt you.

Your current circumstance may be the result of how you dealt with someone who abused you. Your actions may have been your way of getting back at someone for what they did to you. Handling matters in this way does not solve the problem, but rather creates more issues. Regardless of the type of things that are causing you anguish, you can know that there is help for you.

As always, we can look at the example of our perfect Saviour. Hebrews 12:2 says, *Looking unto Jesus the author and finisher of our faith; who for the joy that was set before him endured the cross, despising the shame, and is set down at the right hand of the throne of God.* Have you ever taken the time to look at all that Jesus went through for you? He endured every form of abuse known to man to pay for your sin.

The Bible says that when Jesus took on flesh and came to this earth, he had to leave the joys of heaven for the shame of the cross. Even before He went to the cross, there were many who mocked Him, cursed Him, and treated Him hatefully. This didn't stop Him from completing the purpose for which He came to earth.

Hebrews 12:3 says, *For consider him that endured such contradiction of sinners against himself, lest ye be wearied and faint in your minds.* Whatever we face, if we take time to consider all that Jesus went through for us, it will make our issues pale in comparison. Though Jesus came to die for the sins of the world, He was not well received. Many rejected Him then and many still reject Him today.

Do you know that Jesus has the power to cleanse your mind of things that torment you? Consider Psalm 119:9: *Wherewithal shall a young man cleanse his way? by taking heed thereto according to thy word.* There is power in the Word of God. Jesus can wash and cleanse your mind to the point where your mind can be freed from these troubling experiences.

Let's suppose the thing that plagues you is your own actions. You may have done something that you never imagined you would do. Your actions could have been the result of using drugs or alcohol, or simply just the result of bad decisions.

If you have trusted Christ, He has forgiven you of all your sins. When you sin against God, you can take those sins to Him, and He promises to forgive when you confess. 1 John 1:9 says, *If we confess our sins, he is faithful and just to forgive us our sins, and to cleanse us from all unrighteousness.* What a wonderful promise! What a wonderful God!

God can give you a mind that is in perfect peace. Isaiah 26:3 says, *Thou wilt keep him in perfect peace, whose mind is stayed on thee: because he trusteth in thee.* When we keep our minds focused on the Lord, He can give us His perfect peace.

The devil wants to bring up all our wrongdoings. Remind yourself that God has forgiven you. You can even remind the devil of this fact when he tries to haunt you with things from your past.

If the things you are dealing with mentally are the results of someone else's action, you can forgive them, just as Christ has forgiven you. Some things may seem impossible to forgive, but they are not. Think of all the sins you have committed against the Lord, and yet you've been forgiven. You will find such freedom when you forgive those who have wronged you.

You don't have to live in bondage to these things, but you can have freedom through Christ. Then allow God to use what you've been through to help someone else. As hard as it may seem, you can thank God for the wrongs you have endured, considering all the wrongs Jesus endured for you.

This will not be easy, especially initially, but many have found true victory by doing so. 1 Thessalonians 5:18 says, *In every thing give thanks: for this is the will of God in Christ Jesus concerning you.* You've heard it said before, "Give it to God." That's where you'll find peace and freedom.

Daily Reading

Romans 8:6, 12:2; Ephesians 4:23; Philippians 4:7

Philippians 2:5 – *Let this _____ be in you, which was also in _____ Jesus:*

2 Timothy 1:7 – *For _____ hath not given us the spirit of _____; but of _____, and of _____, and of a sound _____.*

LESSON 27

The Blame Game

No one likes to be blamed for things, especially when it is something we did not do. We've all played the little trick where you do something to another person and then conveniently disappear, making that person blame someone else for your actions. It can be very hard for the innocent person who has been blamed to convince others that he or she is innocent.

One of the oldest games in the book is the blame game. It was literally around in the Garden of Eden. Adam blamed God and Eve for his sin. Genesis 3:12 says, *And the man said, The woman whom thou gavest to be with me, she gave me of the tree, and I did eat.* He blamed Eve but prefaced this blame by reminding God that He gave Eve to him. Eve then blamed the serpent.

This game is also one of the most popular games ever played. It has been used by all of us and we are all quite skilled at playing it.

If you were asked why your circumstances today are as they are, would you play the blame game? I understand that injustices do happen. There have been numerous stories that made national news where people spent a good portion of their lives locked up for something they didn't do. You must take ownership when your circumstances are the result of your own actions.

If you play the blame game, you will find that you will always be the loser. If you are blaming someone else for where you are in life today, you are a loser in this game. The person you are blaming also loses. The only winner in the blame game is the devil.

In the Bible in 1 Samuel 15, God had told the king (Saul) to go to the city of Amalek and to destroy everything in it. Once Saul got to the city, he decided that instead of obeying God, he would destroy some things, but he would keep the best things and not destroy them.

Saul pretended that he had obeyed the Lord's commandment. When the prophet Samuel approached him about his sin, Saul immediately blamed the people who were with him. Verse 15 says, *And Saul said, They have brought them from the Amalekites: for the people spared the best of the sheep and of the oxen, to sacrifice unto the LORD thy God; and the rest we have utterly destroyed.* Saul even claimed that what he had kept back was to be used in sacrifice to God.

Bear in mind, Saul was the king. He was in charge of everyone. He could have stopped them from disobeying God, but he had a part in this too. Because of his sin, God had him replaced as king. Blaming others never turns out well for us. It only creates more problems.

King David was the next king to rule after Saul. At one point during his reign, he was approached by the prophet Nathan for his wrongdoing. Notice how he responded in 2 Samuel 12:13: *And David said unto Nathan, I have sinned against the LORD. And Nathan said unto David, The LORD also hath put away thy sin; thou shalt not die.*

What did he do when he was confronted about his sin? He took ownership and admitted that he had sinned. This is exactly what we need to do.

When you mess up, don't try to point the finger at someone else to make yourself look good. Admit your wrong and make it right, with God and others. This is how you can find freedom from the blame game.

Daily Reading

2 Samuel 12:7-13

1 John 1:9 – *If we _____ our _____, he is _____ and _____ to _____ us our _____, and to _____ us from _____ unrighteousness.*

According to this verse, what is the first step to getting forgiveness? _____ our sins.

LESSON 28

Don't Come Whining to Me!

We've all had those experiences as children when our parents try to instruct us on something that they know is not a good idea, but we are convinced that it is. We hear the warnings and cautions, but our minds think we know best.

After many attempts at trying to get us to listen, the parents may say, "Go ahead, but don't come whining to me later," knowing what the outcome will be. After we go through with our intentions, we end up coming back and crying to our parents. They may not offer us the sympathy we want because they already tried to get us to listen.

Proverbs 1 describes wisdom's appeal to us to seek after it. Wisdom calls out for those who will listen, trying to get us to hear reproof and get the instruction that wisdom provides.

God is the source of wisdom. He calls to us, but often, we refuse. We pay no attention to Him trying to interest us in getting wisdom. Many times, we don't want anything to do with God until we need something from Him. Then we want to come crying to Him for His help.

It is unfortunate for us that we run from God until we get in a situation where we have no one else but Him. We don't realize how desperately we need Him until we are desperate.

God tells us in Proverbs 1 that when He tries to get our attention and draw us to Him and we refuse Him, there will come a time when we need Him and He will turn our own actions back on us.

Listen to these words from Proverbs 1:26: *I also will laugh at your calamity; I will mock when your fear cometh.* Verse 28 of the same chapter says, *Then shall they call upon me, but I will not answer; they shall seek me early, but they shall not find me.*

Imagine God not being there for you in your hour of need. God is merciful and gives you many chances to seek Him, but He will not allow you to take advantage of Him. You will not ignore God and not seek Him, and then think He will come running to your rescue when your life is falling apart.

Seek the Lord now while you have the chance. You have no excuse to not get close to God. If you don't attempt to get close to Him now, it is highly unlikely that you will seek Him later. There will always be something standing in the way.

You need God now more than ever. It is to your advantage to get close to Him. You and your family can benefit when you get close to the Lord.

Please don't waste the opportunity you have to have a good relationship with the Lord. How much better things can be for you when you have actively been seeking the Lord!

Daily Reading

Proverbs 1:24-33

According to verse 28, God will not _____ those who have refused Him and then call on Him for help.

Verse 31 tells us that if we choose not to seek the Lord, we will eat of the _____ of our own _____.

Isaiah 55:6 – _____ *ye the* _____ *while he may be*_____, *call ye upon him while he is* _____:

LESSON 29

How to Handle Rejection

Have you ever been playing a game where everyone who wants to play lines up so teams can be chosen? If you are athletic and those picking the teams know your abilities, this is no big deal to you. But when you may be lacking in athleticism or no one knows your abilities, it can be quite humiliating to be the last one picked, or worse yet, to not get picked at all. Being left on the sidelines when everyone else is playing can leave you feeling rejected.

What about when you're rejected because of your actions? You may have made some bad decisions that have caused those closest to you to reject you. They may not want anything else to do with you. If you are a repeat offender, that can cause the rejection to be even worse.

When your family has rejected you because of something you have done, possibly on more than one occasion, how do you deal with it? They may not want you coming around at all.

You must understand that Jesus knows all about what it is like to be rejected. However, He was not rejected because of His actions or because of sinful doings. He was despised and rejected primarily because of His teachings.

Even the religious leaders hated Him. Luke 9:22 says, *Saying, The Son of man must suffer many things, and be rejected of the elders and chief priests and scribes, and be slain, and be raised the third day.* Yes, Jesus (the Son of man) knows what it is like to experience rejection.

Isaiah 53:3 says, *He is despised and rejected of men; a man of sorrows, and acquainted with grief: and we hid as it were our faces from him; he was despised, and we esteemed him not.* There were many who did not accept Christ then, and many today reject Him.

Whatever heartache you may be experiencing because of feelings of rejection, know that Jesus understands. You can go to Him with your burdens, and He can help you through what you are facing.

Be willing to accept responsibility for your actions. Admit your wrongs to God and take it a step further and be willing to attempt to make things right with those you have wronged. Let them know you are sorry and that you will do all you can to better yourself. Then keep your word and ask God to help you to change your ways.

When others reject you, remind yourself that God loves you in a way that no one else can. Jeremiah 31:3 says, *The LORD hath appeared of old unto me, saying, Yea, I have loved thee with an everlasting love: therefore with lovingkindness have I drawn thee.*

Most people have a conditional love. They will love us if we treat them right and love them as we should, but when we do wrong, that love may falter and waver. This is not the case with the love of God. Despite our sinfulness, He never stops loving us. Remind yourself of the never-ending love of God.

Daily Reading

John 1:11; Psalm 27:10; Romans 8:31

Write out one of the above verses that can help you the most when dealing with rejection.

LESSON 30

Overcoming Issues with Self-Esteem

How many times have you thought you had it all together with your appearance only to find that when you looked in the mirror, something was terribly lacking? Maybe you'd been around people all day and when you checked the mirror, there was lipstick on your teeth. You wonder how long it had been there, how many people noticed, and worse yet, who didn't care enough to tell you.

It's always a good idea to make use of the mirror. Many times, when we don't, we find ourselves in some pretty embarrassing situations. We can save ourselves the embarrassment by taking time to evaluate ourselves.

The mirror is designed to help you see yourself. You don't use a mirror so you can see how someone else looks. It is for you.

It is very unwise to compare ourselves with others, whether in appearance, social standing, or other factors. 2 Corinthians 10:12 says, *For we dare not make ourselves of the number, or compare ourselves with some that commend themselves: but they measuring themselves by themselves, and comparing themselves among themselves, are not wise.*

We can always find someone who we can compare ourselves with to make ourselves look better than they are. Maybe they have something in their past that we don't, so we elevate ourselves above them. We then want to look down on them, thinking ourselves to be above them. This is pride and it is wrong.

Proverbs 16:18 says, *Pride goeth before destruction, and an haughty spirit before a fall.* Being proud of yourself and looking down on others will bring destruction to you. A haughty spirit (a proud attitude) goes before a fall.

I've heard the true statement often, "If you think you are, you're not." If you think you're better, smarter, prettier—you name it—you're not!

Don't get consumed with what others think of you. What does God think of you? Just as looking in the mirror helps you see yourself as you really are, the Word of God can help you see yourself as God sees you.

The Word of God can reveal even what your heart is like. No one else can see your heart, yet spending time in the Bible can not only show you what's in your heart, but it can also be used to give you a right heart.

When you begin to read God's Word, it will change your life. His Word will be like a mirror, showing you how you really are and teaching you what to do to correct the flaws.

The Bible can even help you when you've lost your self-worth. It can remind you of your worth to God. Psalm 139:14 says, *I will praise thee; for I am fearfully and wonderfully made: marvellous are thy works; and that my soul knoweth right well.*

God says about you that you are fearfully and wonderfully made. You are a marvelous work of His. This should really encourage you when the devil and others try to convince you that you are worthless and that you'll never amount to anything.

Rather than trying to lift yourself up above others, allow God to humble you and show you where you need His help. Consider

Proverbs 29:23: *A man's pride shall bring him low: but honour shall uphold the humble in spirit.* Let the Word of God be the mirror for your life.

Daily Reading

Philippians 2:3-4; James 4:6; Matthew 23:12

Write out 2 Corinthians 10:12 in the space below and let it be a reminder not to compare yourself with others.

BONUS LESSON

Keeping Your Relationship with God Strong

Although you have reached the end of this devotional, I trust that it will not be the end of your time in God's Word. Your relationship with God is meant to be constantly growing.

Think of a newborn baby. The baby starts out one hundred per cent dependent on his parents. As the baby grows from an infant to a toddler and beyond, he begins to get independent in many ways.

The Bible terminology for a person accepting Christ is being "born again."

This is not a physical birth, but a spiritual birth. Just as a newborn needs milk to grow, a new Christian needs God's Word to grow and develop.

God expects us to grow in our relationship with Him. This happens as we daily get in the Bible and allow God to give us nourishment through the Word.

A newborn baby that is not being given milk will have issues with growth. In like manner, if you are a "baby Christian" just getting started out and you are not in God's Word, you will not grow as God desires for you to. You will be lacking in spiritual maturity.

This devotional is just a tool to get you started reading God's Word and to help you to see the importance of doing this daily.

You've seen how the layout works. It is meant to be simple so you can continue to read and get things from the Bible on your own.

Here are some simple things for you to do to help you grow as a Christian.

Daily Bible Reading

Spend time every day in God's Word. We make sure our physical bodies are fed every day and usually several times a day. The same should be true of us spiritually. Don't let a day pass when you don't read the Bible. You need the Lord!

Your physical well-being is important, but even more so is your spiritual well-being. Don't neglect to spend time with the Lord. If you don't spend time with God now, you won't do it later. Now is the time!

Have a specific time when you read the Bible. It is best to begin your days with the Lord, putting Him first. Matthew 6:33 says, *But seek ye first the kingdom of God, and his righteousness; and all these things shall be added unto you.* You will never go wrong by putting the Lord first.

Before you begin reading, pray and ask God to help you understand His Word. The King James Version is written on a 5th grade reading level. Don't use the excuse that you just don't understand the Bible. Of course, there will be things that you read that you won't understand, but don't use that as a reason not to read at all.

Ask God to give you one thing from your Bible reading to help you for the day. Write down the thought that God teaches you. You can use this to give you encouragement when you need it.

Prayer

Once you've spent time in the Word, take some time to pray. Begin by thanking God for His blessings on your life. There is so much for all of us to be thankful for. Have a time where you confess your sins to God. This is a daily process since we fail Him every day.

Pray for needs and requests—your own and your loved ones. Praying for those you love is one of the best and most powerful things you can do for them.

Grow in your relationship with God. You are where you are for a reason. Choose to make the most with your time and get closer to God. If you want God to get close to you, it begins by you choosing to get close to Him.

Daily Reading

2 Timothy 3:16; Matthew 22:29; Luke 24:45; Psalm 119:9-11

1 Peter 2:2 – *As newborn _____, desire the sincere _____ of the _____, that ye may _____ thereby:*

Suggested Bible Reading

The book of Proverbs has 31 chapters. Most months have either 30 or 31 days. You can read the chapter of Proverbs that coincides with the date of the month. For example, if today is August 4th, read Proverbs chapter 4.

Read in the book of Psalms. There are 150 chapters in this book. Read daily from this book until you complete the entire book. If you read and nothing touches your heart, keep reading. God may have a treasure waiting for you!

About the Author

After working for several years in various church ministries, Trina Carson developed a burden to provide biblical material to encourage ladies. This devotional is the result of working with women on a weekly basis, recognizing common struggles among them, and studying to provide biblical help for overcoming problem areas.

For additional helps or to contact the author,
Email Trina Carson at faithworksbytrina@gmail.com.

Made in the USA
Middletown, DE
17 July 2022